Original title:
How to Live Without Knowing the Why

Copyright © 2025 Creative Arts Management OÜ
All rights reserved.

Author: Julian Prescott
ISBN HARDBACK: 978-1-80566-169-6
ISBN PAPERBACK: 978-1-80566-464-2

Finding Joy in the Mystery

In a world where questions dance,
I trip on answers, take a chance.
With a wink and a silly grin,
I toss my doubts into the bin.

Life's a puzzle, piece by piece,
Finding joy, my own release.
Like socks that vanish in the wash,
I chase the laughs, my heart's a swash.

Footprints on the Unknown Shore

Waves of wonder crash and crest,
I leave my footprints, that's the jest.
With every splash, I shout hooray,
The tide will take my doubts away.

Seagulls giggle overhead,
As I dance where no one tread.
With sandy toes and wild delight,
I face the waves, ready for flight.

Uncharted Waters of Existence

Sailing seas without a map,
Each wave a giggle, each swell a clap.
The compass spins, it's quite absurd,
But hey, I'm off! Just feel the word.

With jellyfish and bobbing foam,
I surf the chaos, make it home.
Life's a boat adrift on whim,
Let's toast to tides, glasses brim!

Breathing Through the Disquiet

In the quiet, I find my song,
As worries waft, I dance along.
Crisp air tickles my nose with glee,
Each breath a chuckle, wild and free.

With stress like sweaters, snugly tight,
I unravel threads with all my might.
Life's a carnival, full of quirks,
I ride the laughter, toss my smirks.

Echoes of a Thoughtful Heart

In a world of endless why,
I just shrug and wave goodbye.
Like a cat who chases tails,
Or a ship lost in gales.

Toast burns, but I laugh loud,
I dance, even when not proud.
Mysteries swirl in my mug,
Life's a puzzle, not a rug.

A frog leaps, what's the fuss?
I'll jump too, join the circus.
No need for answers or clues,
Just some joy and silly shoes.

With questions buzzing in my ear,
I sip my tea, and have a beer.
Life's a dance, join the spin,
No need to question where or when.

In the Garden of the Unfathomable

Plants whisper their secret tales,
Yet I pluck weeds, as life prevails.
Bees don't ask why they hum,
They just buzz, and that's their drum.

Sunflowers stretch toward the sky,
While I sit back, and wonder why.
Rabbits hop without a care,
I might join them, if I dare.

Watering cans don't have rules,
They simply splash—oh, how it drools!
In this patch of green delight,
We laugh through the day and night.

Let the veggies grow quite tall,
I'll find my joy in the sprawl.
With every bloom, I'll take a seat,
Life is funny with its beat.

A Life Unscripted

Woke up one day, took a leap,
Dreamt of rivers, lost in sleep.
Pancakes flipped, oh what a sight,
But they flew off in mid-flight.

Coffee spills without a doubt,
Now I'm wide awake, no pout.
The cat chuckles, gives a wink,
Life's a stage, with no ink.

Plans go awry like a song,
But I dance along, can't go wrong.
A rollercoaster, ups and downs,
With silly hats and goofy frowns.

Take missteps on this path ahead,
Trip on feelings, laugh instead.
Like a clown with painted face,
Unscripted joys, life's embrace.

The Melody of Questions

In the air, the questions play,
With a tune that fades away.
Like a dog who tilts its head,
I just grin instead of dread.

Whistles float on gentle breeze,
Humming tunes as I feel ease.
Why do socks love to hide?
I just laugh, take it in stride.

Clouds drift by, no answers clear,
Yet I chuckle, full of cheer.
Let the whims dance in the air,
Life's a jest, swing without care.

Every puzzle brings a smile,
I'll embrace the quirky style.
With a wink and silly cheer,
I'll face each day without fear.

Unspoken Threads of Existence

In the morning, toast flies wide,
Jam on my shirt, oh what a ride!
Coffee spills, like dreams awry,
Laughing at fate, I'm still not shy.

Every question, dressed in fun,
Wigs on chairs, our lives are spun.
Why's the cat in a top hat now?
Just roll with it, take a bow!

Growth in the Absence of Clarity

Tickle the pickle, dance with doubt,
Lemons speak; what's this about?
In the garden, weeds can play,
Sunshine giggles, brings the day.

Chasing shadows, join the line,
Bumblebees buzz, oh that's divine!
No GPS in the park's great maze,
Let's misplace all those serious ways!

Letters to the Distant Stars

Stars don't reply, they're just too bright,
Dancing through space, avoiding fright.
I wrote them all, it took a while,
Got ink on my nose, but hey, that's style!

Messages float on cosmic streams,
Universe giggles at our dreams.
Could it be true, a comical view?
Not knowing why, but still feeling new!

Passing Clouds of Thought

Clouds drift by, in foolish haste,
Thoughts like bubbles, can't be replaced.
Why is the sky trying to make us laugh?
Lightning stuns, but it's all a gaffe!

Grab a feather, tickle the rain,
Dance in puddles, ignore the pain.
Life's a riddle with no real key,
Laugh with the clouds; they don't charge a fee!

The Taste of Impermanence

Life's a pie that never stays,
Each piece served in funny ways.
Grab the slice, don't think it through,
Moments vanish, who knew it too?

Sweet flavors dance, they twirl and spin,
Like socks that vanish in a bin.
Taste the chaos, savor the ride,
Embrace the mess, let nonsense abide.

Wondering Along the Winding Road

I wandered down a twisty lane,
Where ducks wore hats and sang in vain.
Each turn a giggle, a silly sight,
Life's a puzzle, not black and white.

A raccoon juggles, the squirrels can dance,
Chasing odd dreams as if by chance.
With every bump, more laughs we score,
On this strange path, who needs a map anymore?

Moments of Joy Amid Confusion

Lost in thought, like socks in a wash,
Happiness sneaks in with a little posh.
A cat in boots, a frog in a suit,
Life's a circus, and we're all root-toot!

Confused yet cheerful, we dance in a line,
Wobbling and laughing, oh isn't it fine?
Moments bubble like soda pop fizz,
In this riddle called life, let's just be whiz!

The Art of Letting Go

Like balloons that float, then drift away,
We cling so tight to our worries each day.
Yet when we release, oh what a sight,
Freedom dances in sheer delight!

So toss your thoughts like confetti in air,
Let them flutter with style and flair.
Embrace the giggles, don't hold them tight,
In the art of release, we find our light!

Sipping Tea with the Unknown

I brew my tea with mystery,
Leaves of doubt and glee.
As I sip, the world may spin,
Laughing at the mess I'm in.

A spoon of sugar, quite a twist,
Sweeten chaos, make a list.
Life's absurd and so bizarre,
Yet here I am, a shining star.

Lizards dance around my cup,
Whiskers twitch, they never stop.
In every sip, a riddle hides,
With laughter, uncertainty abides.

So cheers to tea and antics bold,
In this mystery, I'm consoled.
Who knows what's waiting in the night?
Yet I sip on, feeling light.

Threads of Fate Intertwined

With tangled yarn, I weave my fate,
Knots of laughter, threads await.
Do I ever know the plan?
Ah, the thrill of this strange span.

A sock turned hat, a scarf with flair,
I wear my choices, unaware.
Life's a game of mismatched socks,
I dance to tunes the universe knocks.

In every twist, a chuckle waits,
As I defy the boring fates.
Beneath the stars, I spin my tales,
With giggles as my only sails.

So let me weave, and let it be,
A web of joy, absurdity.
For in the chaos, I shall find,
The threads of life, although unlined.

Searching through the Mist

I wander through a foggy scene,
With rubber boots and jelly beans.
What lies ahead is quite a mess,
Confusion wears a silly dress.

Each step I take, the ground may shift,
A game of chance, a zany gift.
Do I seek a pot of gold?
Or just the stories, brave and bold?

Through misty paths and giggles bright,
I stumble forth, no end in sight.
The questions linger, dance around,
Like socks alive, they can't be found.

Yet in this fog, I find my cheer,
For laughter echoes, loud and clear.
What's wrong with wandering, you say?
I'll laugh at life, come what may!

The Courage to Wander

With a map that's upside down,
I strut along, the silliest clown.
Turn left, turn right, or maybe straight?
Who needs directions? It's all first-rate!

I greet the sun with a cheerful grin,
While ducks quack secrets from within.
The trees gossip and tease with flair,
As I skip lightly through fresh air.

Who knows what's waiting just ahead?
A talking cat or maybe a bed?
Life is a ride on a roller-coaster,
With every twist, I'm a bolder roaster.

So here's to courage, bliss, and cheer,
With every step, I shed my fear.
In the dance of doubt, I find my song,
For wandering's fun, where I belong!

Riddles of the Invisible

In a land of upside-down, we stroll,
Where questions dance, and answers roll.
The sun wears shades, the moon wears a hat,
Chasing shadows, imagine that!

We tiptoe on clouds, and giggle at fate,
Eating spaghetti from a big ole plate.
Why not? We ask, as we twirl in a spin,
Life's a riddle, let the fun begin!

With socks on our hands and hats on our feet,
We juggle our laughter, a silly feat.
The ducks in the park are quacking with glee,
In this wacky world, we just let it be!

So raise a toast with your upside-down drink,
To mysteries wrapped in a secret wink.
Dance in the chaos, embrace the unknown,
For in the laughter, we find our own throne.

Joy in the Journey Undefined

We stroll through life on a wobbly road,
With a skip and a hop, we lighten the load.
Why this? Why that? We chuckle aloud,
In our pants made of clouds, we prance like a crowd.

With jellybean dreams and whimsy in air,
We skip over puddles with a curious flair.
The compass spins round, a dance in our heads,
Mapping our journey on cotton candy threads.

Tickle the stars, pull the moon's cheek,
Tomorrow is silly, and today is unique.
We loop in the loop, with a grin on our face,
Finding joy in the blur, heart racing in place!

So let's not plan, just wander at will,
Life's mystery box is a thrill-seeking thrill.
In the chaos we flourish, in the giggle we find,
The joy in the journey, the puzzle unlined.

Gathering Stars of Hope

In the night, we dance and sway,
Collecting dreams that drift away.
Laughter echoes, stars align,
Chasing wishes, all divine.

Life's a game of peek-a-boo,
With questions hanging in the blue.
Skip the map, just bring some cheer,
Let the whimsy lead us here.

A jester's hat, on wobbly head,
With silly thoughts, we make our bed.
Slipping on the cosmic floor,
Why, though? Who knows? Let's explore!

In chaos lies a hidden jest,
The why is just a curious quest.
We'll giggle at confusion's sting,
And dream of what tomorrow brings.

The Silence Between the Notes.

Whispers linger on the breeze,
Notes unwritten, just to tease.
Dance in silence, leap in fret,
Music's sweetness, no regret.

Bouncing beats in funky shoes,
Tickle truths that we can't choose.
Why not hum a clueless tune?
Let's serenade the silly moon!

Sipping tea on whirly swings,
Where no one knows the funny things.
Questions hang like laundry dry,
While we laugh and wonder why.

A magpie's cackle, sheer delight,
In the quiet, take that flight.
Skip the notes, just feel the vibe,
In the pause, our hearts imbibe.

Silent Questions

Questions bubble like soda pop,
Fizzing out, we'll never stop.
Riding waves of silly thought,
In the chaos, laughter's caught.

Like a cat that chases tails,
Seeking sense in wind-blown trails.
Why not smile with goofy glee?
What's the answer? Let it be!

Cactus hugs and rubber ducks,
Life's a maze of funny luck.
In the mystery, we shall roam,
Face the silly unknown home.

Questions dive, then skip and roll,
Between the lines, we find our soul.
Laugh it off, and just embrace,
The merry dance of time and space.

In the Shadow of Answers

In shadows, answers play hide and seek,
Tickling thoughts, they scatter and leak.
Why be serious? It's more fun,
To skip and twirl under the sun!

Giggles chase the fading light,
Where questions leap into the night.
Silly riddles twist and bend,
In the laughter, we transcend.

Like a puppy chasing its tail,
Reveling in the clueless trail.
Footprints lead to nowhere known,
In the giggles, we have grown.

So join the dance with playful glee,
Let the mystery set you free.
In shadows, we can laugh and play,
For in the silence, dreams will stay.

Journeys Without Maps

Wander the world with a silly grin,
Forget the route, let the chaos begin.
Every twist and turn, just roll with the show,
Laugh at the signs, let your spirit flow.

Dance with the clouds, jest with the breeze,
Why worry about plans? Just do what you please.
Lost in a giggle, the world flips around,
Who needs a compass when joy can be found?

Step on that puddle, embrace the splatter,
Life's a grand joke; don't sweat the chatter.
Get sidetracked by ducks or a funky old hat,
As long as it's funny, nothing's the matter.

In the end, it's a circus under the sun,
Forget the details; it's all meant for fun.
Every misstep, a tale to create,
With laughter as fuel, there's no room for fate.

Threads of Existence

Life's a patchwork, all jumbled and spry,
Stitching the moments that flit and fly.
With each quirky thread, just weave and unwind,
A tapestry wild, too vibrant to bind.

Stumble through life with mismatched socks,
Chasing the countdown of ticking clocks.
What's the point when the rug keeps slipping?
Hang on for the ride; keep giggling, not tripping.

Every thread tangles; don't take it to heart,
Each snarl tells a tale, an unusual art.
Laugh at the mess, it's what makes us whole,
A stomach full of chuckles is a happy soul.

In the fabric of whimsy, we find our glue,
The silly and sweet, chasing life's brew.
Getting lost in the weave might paint you a clown,
But in this grand quilt, wear your joy as a crown.

Chasing Moments, Not Answers

Why seek perfection in every blink?
Grab that wild moment; it's quicker than you think.
Each chuckle a gem, tossed into the air,
Forget the big picture, just stop and stare.

A dance with the whims, a hop in the park,
Questions give chase, but we're running in the dark.
Life's an absurdity; don't try to decode,
Like a cat in a box, no one cares where you go.

Time's a slippery fish, wriggling in your net,
Catch it with laughter, and don't break a sweat.
Chase after the giggles; let the why be loose,
A treasure of chuckles is your golden juice.

In the carnival of chaos, we spin and we sway,
Feeling the joy in the mess of the day.
Embrace the wild ride, just let the fun start,
In a game with no rules, seek out your heart.

The Beauty of Just Being

Why fret over reasons when here we are now?
A toast to the absurd, let's take a bow!
In pajamas or crowns, let laughter ignite,
Life's an odd party; it's always just right.

With each breath we take, so absurdly true,
What matters is being; not searching for clues.
Stumble and tumble, trip over the bliss,
In the chaos of now, what a silly twist!

Wobble like jelly, giggle down the street,
Chase after the sun, the jester's retreat.
Embrace all the quirks, make a joyful decree,
In the art of just being, we're wild and we're free.

The world is a stage, and we're all in the cast,
Forget about reasons; just have a blast.
In the dance of existence, let laughter take flight,
For the beauty of now is our utmost delight.

Conversations with the Infinite

I asked the stars for guidance,
They replied with cosmic giggles,
"Life's a circus without a map!"
And the moon just winked, unfazed.

I tried to chat with a cloud,
It drizzled and lost its temper,
"Why so moody, oh fluffy one?"
"I'm just trying to lighten up!"

A tree once whispered secrets,
Its leaves rustled in a breeze,
"Roots know more than you think,"
I pondered and hugged the trunk.

So I dance in the uncertainty,
While laughing at what I can't trace,
Who needs a guide to this mess?
The joy is in each silly step.

Embracing Tomorrow's Mysteries

I woke up with questions dancing,
Like squirrels on a sugar spree,
"What if I change the world today?"
Or what if my toast burns again?

The sun peeked in, all knowing,
"Why so serious, dear little one?"
I chuckled, with crumbs in my beard,
"Guess we'll find out after lunch."

Riding waves of vague possibilities,
I hugged a cactus for good luck,
"Will it prick me or give me many hugs?"
The answer's wrapped in this chaos.

Embracing each strange encounter,
As life throws pies in my face,
Tomorrow's mysteries tickle me,
And I can't help but smile wide.

A Tapestry of Questions

My mind weaves a snug blanket,
Each thread a quirky mystery,
"Why are there socks in the fridge?"
Maybe they're hiding from laundry.

A cat sat regally pondering,
"What if fish could fly someday?"
I laughed, imagining scaly pilots,
"Would they need tiny seatbelts?"

In cafes, I sip philosophy,
While sugar cubes stare back at me,
"Are you sweet or just a facade?"
Oh, life loves to stir the pot!

Though answers hide like shy crickets,
I'll catch them in my silly net,
Each unanswered riddle sparks joy,
In this mad dance of delight.

The Heart's Uncharted Territory

My heart's a mapless wonderland,
With trails that lead to nowhere fast,
"Where's the picnic or the treasure?"
I just giggle and roll in grass.

A whisper flirted with my thoughts,
"If you follow the ripe mango scent?"
"Do I get lost or find a feast?"
Either way, I'm hungry for fun!

I sought the meaning of dancing,
But the music just twirled and played,
"Is it steps or just silly flailing?"
As long as everybody's laughing!

Through ups and downs and odd detours,
This journey's not meant for the sane,
I'll navigate with a goofy grin,
And trust joy aches when it rains.

A Story Without a Title

Once I lost my sock in the wash,
It danced with glee, a daring posh.
I searched high and low, my patience thin,
Yet the missing pair still won't let me win.

The cat just yawned and shrugged it off,
While I spun tales of sneaky cloth.
Maybe it's off, embarking on fate,
While I'm here pondering, simply irate.

On days the toast burns, I laugh and sigh,
Perhaps my bread wants to learn to fly.
In chaos unseen, I find my way,
And question less what might go astray.

So here's my tale, with no ending in sight,
My sock will return, maybe just at night.
Life's odd twists, well, they can amuse,
In silly stories, I'll always choose.

Trusting the Unseen

My keys have a flair for hide-and-seek,
Under the couch, or in the cheek.
They laugh at my panic, oh the nerve,
Yet somehow, I find them - such a curve!

The toast? It flips with a flip of fate,
Landing butter-side down, it can't wait.
It's a conspiracy, I just know,
Even the butter's in on the show.

Trusting the unseen is quite a gig,
Like betting on turtles in a card game rig.
You cheer for the slow ones, think they'll swerve,
Yet they plod ahead with unyielding nerve.

So here I stand, with a chuckle so bright,
Life's a funny dance—a whimsical flight.
In unseen places, surprises appear,
And that's how I wander, without a fear.

Glimmers of Hope in the Dark

In the depths of night, a fridge light stirs,
Gathering courage, I make my purrs.
Oh, leftover pizza, my dear old friend,
In the dark, you sparkle, as taste buds lend.

A lost pen lies under books so tall,
With treasures trapped like a ragged brawl.
I dig for the ink, it's quite the quest,
Each scribble whispers, 'You are blessed!'

In shadows, I fumble, searching for glee,
My cat's cold stare says, "Why bother, flee?"
Yet I find laughter in odd little sparks,
Glimmers of hope, like bright little larks.

Through every stumble, I find my way,
Laughter in night light, keeping gloom at bay.
In the dark's embrace, I will dance without fright,
Finding joy in the chaos, a comedic delight.

Threads of Fate and Fortune

I tried to sew buttons on with flair,
Yet each one wobbles, a comical pair.
Like a circus act, they wobble and spin,
Oh, the looks they give, where do I begin?

When fate throws fabric, I zig and zag,
Creating a quilt of the life I drag.
Stitch after stitch, I ponder this art,
With threads of fortune, I play my part.

Each misstep's a dance, a rhythm so sweet,
Even when my shoe's yelling, 'Try a retreat!'
Yet onward I go, with a grin ear to ear,
For fate wears a costume; it's all rather queer.

So here's to the threads, tangled and bright,
Woven in laughter, with each error, delight.
In a world of mayhem, I find joy's embrace,
Trusting the dance in this curious space.

The Freedom of Ambivalence

Woke up today, what's the plan?
Coffee, or toast? Or just a can?
Dance like no one sees me sway,
Laugh at life's odd games we play.

Chose the road less traveled on,
Took a left turn, then was gone.
Might be lost, but that's just fine,
Life's a joke and I'm the punchline.

The menu's vast, I'll take a bite,
Of mystery stew, served just right.
Swirling thoughts, a merry jive,
In this chaos, feel so alive.

Why the fuss, why complain?
Ambivalence runs in my vein.
Floating free on whims and fates,
Just be sure to pass the plates!

Unknown Rivers Flowing

Wandered here without a clue,
Might just swim or build a shoe.
Unknown rivers, what's the fuss?
How far they go? Just ride the bus!

Bubbles rise, then pop with glee,
What's beneath? I'll wait and see.
Life's a splash, a wild ride,
With questions hidden deep inside.

Grappling thoughts like fish in nets,
Tangled up in all my bets.
Still, I laugh and lose my way,
Tomorrow's light will save the day.

Falling leaves on rivers dance,
Swinging on a strange romance.
Hold my breath, just let it flow,
Grinning wide, no need to know!

Embracing the Blank Canvas

Gaze at white, such empty space,
Splash of colors? Just in case.
Stick to blues, and maybe reds,
Or chartreuse—just see where it leads!

Brush in hand, but what's the play?
Dribbles here, like thoughts in gray.
Each stroke brings a giggle's sound,
Which way to twist, I'm spellbound.

Plans are made but quickly torn,
Like old newspapers, weathered, worn.
On this canvas, let me free,
What's a mistake? It's art, you see!

Embrace the chaos, fear not the stain,
Life's a doodle, drive me insane.
Shouting colors, joyous din,
On this canvas, let's begin!

The Lightness of Letting Go

Dropped my worries on the floor,
Waved goodbye, can't take much more.
Life's balloons, they float away,
Tickle my nose, come out to play.

Chuckling fears, they scurry fast,
What was once heavy, now's a blast.
Let it drift, those thoughts unbound,
In this lightness, joy is found.

Bathrobe on, and hair askew,
Chasing dreams, where's my shoe?
Giggles bubble, skies so blue,
Holding on's for the timid crew.

With each giggle, more I glide,
Life's a dance, come join the ride.
Laugh and twirl, just let it show,
The secret's lightness—let it go!

Life Beyond the Questions

The chicken crossed the road, they say,
But why? Who cares! It's just a play.
Life's odd twists, the jokes that sprout,
In every question, laugh it out.

A squirrel steals my sandwich, oh dear!
Was it for lunch, or just some cheer?
In every moment, a brand-new jest,
With laughter, life's a quirky fest.

Why the moon glows? Who even knows?
It whispers secrets, then slyly goes.
Each shine's a riddle, a giggling ghost,
In the cosmic party, it's always the host.

So dance to the beat of the unknown,
With silly socks and a funny bone.
Life without answers is a wild ride,
So let's hold hands and enjoy the slide!

The Art of Uncertainty

Tiptoeing through life, I lost my shoe,
But hey, it happens, and who knew?
Each misstep's a chance to trip and laugh,
In this grand theater, I'll take a half.

Questions swirl like autumn leaves,
Do I want answers, or just to tease?
With a wink and a nod, I dance away,
As life's absurdities join the play.

Forget the map, I'll draw my own,
A wavy line with ice cream cones.
Navigating chaos with a happy grin,
In every blunder, that's where I win!

So raise your glass, toast the night,
To living oddly, it feels just right.
Uncertainty's the spice, a giggle sweet,
In this grand adventure, let's shake our feet!

Navigating by Stars Unseen

Starships and aliens, oh what a sight!
But wait, is that pizza I smell tonight?
Guided by cravings, the cosmos unknown,
We orbit around snacks, a truth brightly shone.

What's to the left? And what's to the right?
A dance on the edge of sheer delight.
With each silly question, a burst of cheer,
We're flying through life, with our mugs of beer.

Shadows of doubt creep and crawl,
But who needs a plan when you're having a ball?
In the vast universe, I'll twirl and sway,
Navigating laughter in the quirkiest way.

So here's to the stars that twinkle above,
And to all the silly things that we love.
With hope in our hearts and snacks in our hands,
We'll wander this life, it's simply grand!

The Path of Wandering Souls

Wandering down the path with a frown,
I ponder deep things while tripping down.
Who put this rock here? It makes no sense,
Life's a big puzzle with missing fence.

Why do clouds float? And why do they rain?
Like life's little jokes, it's all in the game.
With rubber ducks and dreams so bold,
The silliness of life never gets old.

Chasing butterflies, I slip on goo,
In the grand scheme of things, it's nothing new.
With giggles and snorts, we prance and play,
In this whimsical world, who knows the way?

So let's skip and tumble, just like the breeze,
In a silly dance where laughter's the keys.
With no answers in sight, we'll find our way,
In this glorious chaos, we seize the day!

A Dance in the Unknown

Twirl and spin with no clear aim,
Fumbling lightly, that's the game.
Duck and weave, it's quite absurd,
Shouting excuses, no need for words.

Feet may stumble, joy shall rise,
Waltzing past all the whys and lies.
Giggles erupt in curious sways,
Lost in the whirl, we dance for days.

Mistakes are welcome, in this charade,
Life's just a joke that's perfectly made.
Every fall is a brand new start,
Laughter is truly the best part.

So raise a glass to the great unknown,
In silly circles, we've brightly grown.
A quirky jig, no need for a plan,
Join in the fun, let's all be fans!

The Quiet Embrace of Ambiguity

In a world of riddles, we curl and pout,
Why's just a question that we throw out.
Cups half full, or just full of air,
Let's sip from confusion without a care.

Jellybeans in pockets, that's a good sign,
They'll sweeten the day, no need to align.
What's lost in reason can't ruin the fun,
So let's play ping pong under the sun.

Thoughts like butterflies, flitting away,
Chasing our tails, we'll play this strange way.
With capes of delusion flapping behind,
We'll laugh and roll, leaving logic blind.

So breathe in the chaos, it's quite the thrill,
Dance with the questions, they rattle and chill.
For every answer we stumble upon,
Let's spin in delight—oh, the fun's just begun!

Stepping into Shadows

Shadows lurk in the corners of thought,
Creepy and funny, they're all that we've got.
Tiptoe through whispers, the truth's out to play,
Each step is a giggle, come what may.

No lights are needed when we have our flair,
We dance through the night in this strange, dark air.
Shuffled and muddled, we laugh at the void,
They say 'be careful'—we're just overjoyed!

Tripping on answers we never received,
Stumbling through life, it's all we believe.
In every wrong turn lies a fun little game,
Let's chase the shadows, and giggle the same!

So here's to the journeys, both weird and bright,
Let's step into shadows, and dance in the night.
With no need for reasons, just watch us sway,
In the art of confusion, we'll find our own way!

Embracing the Unanswered

Flip a coin; heads or tails will do,
In this delightful mess, the fun's overdue.
Questions tumble like socks in the wash,
In the mix of absurdity, we truly can't squash.

Let's play leapfrog over thoughts that confuse,
While sipping our drinks, we've little to lose.
Why's that so funny? Who needs a plan?
A riddle awaits the brave and the grand!

Tangled in whimsy, with socks on our hands,
We color outside most of life's little plans.
The map's just a doodle, who needs it anyway?
With charts full of doodles, we'll laugh all day!

So gather your giggles, let chaos inflate,
In the space of 'why not,' we'll happily skate.
For unanswered questions are true friends indeed,
Embracing confusion, we're perfectly freed!

The Unraveled Path

Once I took a stroll and tripped,
Thought I'd find a clue or script.
But all I found were shoes and socks,
And hedgehogs plotting in their docks.

I asked a mushroom for some hints,
It chuckled loud, then winked and squints.
"Just follow me, or wander free,
The why is lost, but look at me!"

A squirrel laughed, "What's in a quest?
The journey's fun; it's quite the jest!"
So off I went, no map or plan,
Each step I took, a wobbly fan.

And now I dance with trees so spry,
They twist and sway, oh me, oh my!
With every fall, I shout, "Hooray!"
For life, it seems, has its own way.

Flickers of Light Among Shadows

In shadows deep, I lit a spark,
While ice cream trucks sang in the park.
The reason's lost, but oh, such fun,
I chased the light, I ran, I spun.

A glowbug flashed, "You seek a sign?"
I simply grinned, "Just passing time."
It danced a jig, then flew away,
While I enjoyed a sunny day.

With every step, I felt more free,
No need to ponder, laugh with glee.
A shadow puppet joined the rhyme,
And whispered, "Life? It's just a clime!"

So here I twirl with all my friends,
Through flickering light, where laughter blends.
No reasons needed, joy's the key,
In this grand show, I'll always be.

A Compass Without Directions

With a compass spinning like a top,
I ventured forth, I'd never stop.
North? South? What does it matter now?
I'll find my way, I'll take a bow!

The squirrels chirp, "You're half a fool!"
I lounge around at Nature's school.
A birdy said with a cheeky grin,
"Come sail with us; we'll scoot and spin!"

My GPS broke; who needs that mess?
In this fine chaos, I find success.
With every twist, a laugh I share,
Forget the path, just breathe the air!

So let's toast to wrong turns made,
In this grand game, we're all okay.
With laughter loud amid the cheer,
We roam the wild — no room for fear!

Dancing with the Fates

I twirled with fate, it was surreal,
In mismatched socks, a funky deal.
"Why am I here?" I asked the breeze,
It whispered, "Dance, do as you please!"

A cat on a fence winked, "Take a chance!
Maybe you'll trip, but join the dance."
With every twirl, confetti flew,
The why became a bright, bold hue.

So I rolled with it, a chuckle loud,
Lost in the crowd, feeling quite proud.
With jumbled steps, we spun in rings,
Celebrating life and all its flings!

Each stumble led me to a friend,
In this wacky dance, there's no end.
I laugh and sway, my fate's in hand,
For life's a fiesta, just take a stand!

In the Embrace of Paradox

In a world of questions, I skip and sway,
Chasing shadows that dance in the fray.
With a grin full of mischief, I leap with glee,
Why do I do this? Well, who must we be?

Round and round, I twirl in confusion,
Living life like a bright contradictions.
The answers are tangled, a hilarious sight,
Yet I'm laughing so hard, I'm feeling alright!

When the sky rains secrets, I wear a big hat,
With raindrops like jewels, they splatter and splat.
I duck and I dodge, in a comical chase,
For wisdom's elusive, but I'm in the race!

Oh, the riddles we clutch in our crazy quest,
Every quirk and each quirk, just adds to the jest.
I giggle at fate, it's quite the charade,
Because who needs a map when you're hand in hand with parades!

Solitude of the Seeking Heart

In the quiet of asking, I trip on my shoes,
Searching for answers, I'm chasing the blues.
My heart seeks the truth like a hungry little pup,
But it wags with delight: 'Why not just sup?'

On a quest for the meaning, I sip from a cup,
Craving deep thoughts, but I'm stuck in a rut.
I tumble, I fumble, with laughter I shout,
'It's all just a riddle, have you ever thought out?'

In the solitude's comfort, I dance with my doubt,
Each ponderous moment, I laugh, scream, and pout.
With a smile on my face, I know it's a lark,
The heart wanders freely, igniting a spark!

Alone with a thought that bubbles away,
I chase whimsical dreams that choose to betray.
But isn't the folly a marvelous art?
In solitude's laughter, I find my true heart!

A Song in the Silence

In the stillness of night, a tune starts to play,
Notes of confusion just dance in the gray.
I hum to the stars, with laughter unfurled,
What's the rhythm? Just twirls in this world!

Whispers of giggles float under the moon,
Singing of chaos, a joyous cartoon.
Ask the wise owls, they'll crack a sly grin,
As they cackle and chuckle, say, 'Dive right in!'

In silence we scream, oh what a delight,
The melody's funny, despite the moonlight.
For the more that we ponder, the more we can smile,
With each curious question, let's ponder a while!

So let's dance in the quiet, a marvelous spree,
To a song that's unknown, you'll giggle with me.
Unravel the laughter, unlock what's inside,
In songs of confusion, with joy as our guide!

Blossoms of Ambivalence

In the garden of maybes, I wander and strain,
Pondering if sunshine should dance with the rain.
With petals of laughter, I pluck and I tease,
Which flower is right? Oh, let's just appease!

In this tangled bouquet of questions galore,
Dandelions argue with roses, what's more?
Each bloom whispers loudly, 'Do we need a plan?'
I shrug, twirl, and giggle, 'Let's just be a fan!'

Through the thorns of confusion, I wade without fear,
In the lush, vibrant chaos, I find my good cheer.
With ambivalence dancing upon swaying stems,
I embrace all the whims, let's see how it bends!

Oh, the petals of doubt can tickle and tease,
Yet each curious thought becomes a sweet breeze.
In this garden of ours, a whimsical spree,
Let's laugh at the questions and blossom carefree!

A Flame in the Fog

In a world where shadows play,
I dance around in bright dismay.
With laughter loud and worries few,
I juggle thoughts, then drop a shoe.

Muffin crumbs spill, a sweet delight,
I chase them down—oh, what a sight!
A candle flickers in the breeze,
While I trip over my own knees.

Pondering why the sky is blue,
I make a hat from my cat's shoe.
The fog swirls 'round, my brain's a mess,
Yet I strut like royalty in my dress.

With whimsy wrapped around my head,
I skip through life, enough said!
For answers hide in silly games,
While I parade, collecting names.

Still Waters Run Deep

In the pond where ducks play peek,
I ponder life's odd, mystic streak.
Moving stones, they giggle soft,
While I hope my thoughts lift off.

Water lilies float like dreams,
I make wishes, or so it seems.
What's that ripple? Who can tell?
A frog that croaks his secret spell!

Down below where shadows seep,
I stash my secrets, oh so deep.
Yet every leap and silly splash,
Brings forth laughter in a flash.

Still I stare, no answers known,
Embracing chaos in my zone.
Life swirls by, it's quite absurd,
And I keep laughing, undeterred.

Between Questions and Answers

I stand on a seesaw, tipping high,
Balancing truths that float on by.
What's the meaning? I jest and laugh,
While squirrels plot their cunning gaffe.

With questions buzzing like pesky flies,
I swat them down with my playful sighs.
At the crossroads, I flip a coin,
And dance to tunes that life'll anoint.

What makes the world spin 'round at night?
I ask the stars, they sparkle bright.
Yet in their silence, fun prevails,
As I juggle fog while cracking tales.

Between the words, I strut in glee,
For life's a question, just like me.
With nonsense wrapped around my spark,
I'll waddle through the curious dark.

The Sound of Uncertainty

Oh, the sound of a rubber duck,
Quacking truth in a world of luck.
I'm spinning round on a whimsy chair,
While chance throws confetti in my hair.

The tick-tock of questions pound like drums,
Yet in this tune, absurdity hums.
The goldfish wiggles in a glass parade,
While I ponder if socks can be made.

Uncertainty's a wild beast on a spree,
Drinking juice from a cup of mystery.
But every sip tickles my chin,
As I grin, while the questions begin.

So here I sway with a giggling grin,
In the dance of nonsense, I dive in.
Life's a riddle wrapped in delight,
Where laughter echoes through the night.

Embrace the Unseen Path

Woke up this morning, thought I'd try,
Chasing shadows in the bright blue sky.
With socks on my hands and a hat on my feet,
I danced with my toaster, a truly odd treat.

I wave at the clouds, they wave back in jest,
In a world where nonsense reigns as the best.
I juggle my coffee, spill it on the floor,
In this game of life, I laugh and I snore.

I wear mismatched shoes, and that's okay,
Life's a silly song, let's all dance and sway.
With butterflies flying in unison green,
Together we skip, and our joy lights the scene.

So let's forge ahead, with a wink and a grin,
Embrace the unknown, let the adventure begin.
With giggles and chuckles, all worries we'll shed,
On this unseen path, let's follow where led.

Dance with Uncertainty

I twirl like a leaf in the wild autumn breeze,
With squirrels on my feet, oh what a tease!
A tango with chaos, I trip and I spin,
Swinging my doubts like a drum on the chin.

At the edge of confusion, I step on a crank,
In rubbery boots, I hop in the tank.
Why fish for answers when whirlwinds are fun?
I'll be the star of this hilarious run.

In the misty unknown, I slide and I glide,
Waving to reasons as they drift and they hide.
With flops and with flails, and a pie to the face,
This dance of delight is my own little space.

Come join in the fun, let worries be light,
We'll frolic with fate till it's gone out of sight.
In the clumsy of chaos, there's laughter and cheer,
So dance with uncertainty, embrace what is near.

The Art of Living Without Clarity

In a world of questions, I'm lost in the haze,
I wore my pajamas for six sunny days.
With toast for a hat and a coffee surprise,
I chase after answers that twist and disguise.

I'm the painter of skies with a brush made of cheese,
Creating a masterpiece that floats on the breeze.
With each stroke of doubt, my canvas grows wide,
Life's a quirky art show, come join for the ride.

I balance my plate on a juggling bear,
Trying to find meaning in the smell of fresh air.
With giggles and grins, I can clearly see,
The secret to living is wild jubilee.

So I sing without lyrics, dance without shoes,
Making up reasons like I'm playing the blues.
In this zany existence, so vivid, so bright,
The art of just being feels perfectly right.

Whispers in the Void

In the echo of questions, I'm sailing alone,
With a bic pen for compass, and ice cream for throne.
I tiptoe on stardust while counting to four,
Who needs all the answers when joy's at the door?

I shout to the void, and it whispers back 'who?',
A riddle, a gander—maybe just a kangaroo.
With cereal clouds swimming through whimsical skies,
I laugh with the echoes, roll my eyes at the wise.

I stumble on ground made of laughter and mirth,
A playground of nonsense, the land of rebirth.
With paper airplanes sailing through tales yet untold,
Embracing the fun in the chaos, be bold.

So here's to the whispers, the giggles they bring,
We dance with the void, let our choices take wing.
In a tapestry woven with each silly thought,
We find our own rhythm, in the joy that we sought.

Navigating the Unknown

I woke up today, not a single plan,
My coffee was cold, but I did not scram.
The sun was a mystery, shining so bright,
I wore mismatched socks, feeling just right.

I wandered through life like a lost puppy,
My shoes were too big, but I felt all chubby.
With each silly mishap, I laughed out loud,
Finding joy in the chaos, feeling so proud.

The world threw me curves, I just did my dance,
In the swirl of the unknown, I took my chance.
I stumbled and tumbled, but I didn't mind,
For in the absurd, true joy I would find.

So here's to the journey, the wild and the free,
Embracing the nonsense, just let it be!
Lost in my thoughts, wearing a grin,
Who needs the why when the fun's about to begin?

The Comfort of Not Knowing

Woke up with a smile, no clue in sight,
Breakfast was cereal; I can't get it right.
The milk was in shadows, the spoon was a thief,
But hey, who needs reasons when you've got belief?

I wore a bright hat, not quite my style,
Folks stopped and stared, but I said, 'Stop a while!'
In the land of confusion, my heart feels at home,
With no need for a map, just a silly chrome dome.

I tripped on a cat, gave a laugh from my gut,
Kicked up some dust, 'Oh, that's just my strut!'
In life's grand circus, I'm here to play,
Why figure it out? Just enjoy the buffet!

So here's to the days when we're lost in our way,
Finding gold in the odd; it brightens the gray.
Embracing the strange, like a wonderfully show,
In the comfort of not knowing, I steal the show!

A Journey with No Map

Packed all my bags, but forgot my hat,
Wandered in circles, oh silly me, fat!
With each silly step, I called it a twirl,
Dancing to riddles as my mind would unfurl.

No signs to follow, just vibes in the air,
Got lost in a garden, but I didn't care.
Met a wise turtle; we chatted for hours,
Turns out he had jokes, amidst all the flowers.

I tried to find home, but took a long detour,
Found joy in the mishaps, oh, what's a bore?
Every wrong turn brought a giggle or two,
Each path was a riddle, and I solved them anew.

So here's my advice, in case you get stuck,
Sing with the birds, and dance like a duck.
Through the wild unknowns, find humor and cheer,
For no map's ever needed when laughter is near!

Embracing the Unexplainable

Open the fridge, what's that fuzzy thing?
A mystery snack that began to sing!
I poked it with wonder, it giggled a tune,
Life's strange little treasures, like dancing on moon.

The clock struck thirteen, my coffee turned green,
I wore it with pride; now I'm the caffeine queen!
Exploring the odd, not a clue on my side,
In laughter and chaos, let kookiness glide.

Every puzzled moment, an invitation to play,
Bumping into strange folks along the way.
"Why are we here?" they all seem to ask,
I shrug with delight, enjoying the task.

So here's to the quirks, the wild and the fun,
In a world full of questions, let's all just run.
Embrace the unexplainable, wear your best hat,
For life's big riddle ends with a laugh — imagine that!

Driftwood in the Sea of Life

Floating on the waves I go,
No map, no plan, just ebb and flow.
My compass? A gull's laughter bright,
Navigating through day and night.

With barnacles of doubt to wear,
I drift along without a care.
Life's a beach with grains so fine,
I'll sip my seashell drink and dine.

Every tide brings something new,
Like jellyfish dancing with a shoe.
What's the reason? Who could say!
I'm just here to surf and play.

So cheers to chaos on the sea,
For waves and whims set my heart free.
In this flotilla, I shall float,
Driftwood vibes keep me remote.

Living in the Flicker

A candle burns with flickering light,
Its dance is neither wrong nor right.
Why it sways? I've lost the thread,
But I'll toast marshmallows instead.

With shadows bouncing on the wall,
I giggle at the shadows tall.
Questions hover like candles high,
But I just want to munch and sigh.

The clock ticks loud, yet I don't care,
Time's a jester, a silly affair.
I'll trade my worries for a snack,
Laugh at the crumbs that fall and stack.

In this theater of whimsy bright,
Living well is my true delight.
With every flicker, life's a game,
Unraveled puzzles, all the same.

Upon the Fragile Edge

Balancing on life's tightrope line,
Wobbling left, oh so divine.
Why not somersault? Who could know,
The thrill of tipping, what a show!

I wear clown shoes, two sizes too big,
Every step's a comical gig.
With laughter echoing far and wide,
I plunge in joy with arms spread wide.

The ground below might seem so close,
Yet here I dance, a merry dose.
Questions whirl, but I'll just twirl,
Life's absurd, let the laughter unfurl.

So here's to all who dare to tread,
Upon the edge where minds are led.
Fragile, funny, flailing too,
I'll laugh at life, and it laughs back too.

Heartbeats Amidst the Questions

My heartbeats hum a zany tune,
Among the doubts that float like balloons.
Why am I here? A cosmic jest,
But I'm still looking for a quest.

Each thump a riddle, each pause a tease,
I bounce through life with puzzling ease.
Tickle my fancies with whimsy's flair,
A chuckle here, a snicker there.

Questions buzz like bees in spring,
Yet I'm dancing like a dingle-ding.
Embrace the silly in every thrum,
Why ask why when fun's become?

So bring your quirks and let them soar,
Heartbeats giggle, who needs a score?
In laughter's arms, we'll play a while,
Amidst the questions, let's share a smile.

Echoes of Unanswered Prayers

I asked for clarity, got a cat instead,
She stares at walls while I'm in my bed.
With furball wisdom, she laughs away,
While I juggle verses, come what may.

The universe chuckles, a cosmic jest,
Who knew my questions would become a fest?
With a wink and a purr, all burdens lift,
In my pillow fort, I find my gift.

I ponder the meaning with a slice of pie,
While the toaster sings, "Don't ask me why!"
A dance of chaos, the world spins tight,
As I toast to life with my morning bite.

In echoes of laughter, I lose my sense,
Embracing the absurd, my recompense.
Perhaps confusion is the truest art,
With joy in the mess, I take it to heart.

Serendipity in the Everyday

Tripping on sidewalks, I find a dime,
A lucky charm in my clumsy rhyme.
The sun winks at me from behind a cloud,
While birds sing nonsense, joyfully loud.

Coffee spills chaos, drips on my shoe,
I laugh at the mess and sip my brew.
With each little stumble, a treasure awaits,
In the dance of mishaps, I open the gates.

Every wrong turn feels like a treat,
With pizza in hand, life's never complete.
An umbrella flips in the breeze so spry,
While I chase my hat, oh me, oh my!

In the swirl of the mundane, I find delight,
Like a child in a puddle, splashing in flight.
With whimsy and wonder as constant friends,
Every day's a circus, and the laughter never ends.

Finding Peace in the Puzzle

Pieces of life scattered wide,
I try to connect them with foolish pride.
A corner here, a straight edge there,
The picture's a mess—but I don't care.

Jigsaw doubts form a chaotic frame,
As I fit them together, losing the game.
But each quirky shape seems to smile at me,
"Embrace the weirdness, just let it be!"

In mismatched colors and puzzling styles,
I laugh at the effort that swamps my trials.
Every wrong piece is a giggle unfurled,
In my delightful and daft little world.

Finding peace in the jumble I weave,
With grace in the nonsense, I start to believe.
That life isn't perfect, and what does it mean?
Just to dance in the chaos, like an unruly queen.

Floating Through the Fogs of Doubt

In a foggy haze, I drift and sway,
With questions like bubbles, I chase them away.
Clouds of confusion, a whimsical ride,
Like a kite in the tempest, buoyed by the tide.

I fumble through moments, a cartoonish dance,
With my thoughts as the jester, I give them a chance.
The more that I ponder, the more I unwind,
In this circus of doubt, a punchline's defined.

Silliness sprinkles like fairy dust flung,
While I giggle at phantoms that once had me strung.
Each worry dissolves like a mist in the breeze,
And I twirl through uncertainty with whimsical ease.

So here's to the fog, my curious friend,
In the laughter of chaos, my heart will mend.
For every lost question, a riddle unfolds,
In the magic of not knowing, adventure beholds.

The Whisper of a Wandering Soul

When questions swirl and logic bends,
I tie my shoes but forget the ends.
With every step, I lose my way,
Yet dance like it's a bright, new day.

A squirrel asked me for some advice,
I said, "Just chill; life's a roll of dice!"
But he just stared, with tiny paws,
Guess wisdom's never found in jaws.

The clouds above laugh at my plight,
While I juggle thoughts, both dark and light.
If I can't find the map, that's fine,
I'll make a game of the errant line.

So here I wander, in joyful strife,
Pinching the silliness out of life.
With each absurd twist, I embrace the fun,
For in this chaos, I've already won.

A Thread in an Infinite Tapestry

A spider spins without a thought,
What tangled web has fate begot?
I giggle as I weave my dreams,
In patterns strange, life's not as it seems.

My coffee spills, a modern art,
Each splash a stroke, a quirky part.
With every drip, a tale unfolds,
Of random wonders and yarns retold.

I found a sock inside a tree,
Dear nature laughs, what could this be?
Yet in the oddity, I find delight,
A simple thread can spark the night.

So here I sit in threads of fate,
Embracing chaos, it's never too late.
For in each knot and every twist,
Lies the magic that can't be missed.

Dancing at the Edge of Reason

I twirl at dusk, but why I dance?
Perhaps to spark a cosmic chance.
With shoes untied and hair askew,
I cha-cha with the morning dew.

Thoughts leap like frogs in summer's sun,
Each leap a riddle, oh what fun!
Even the moon shakes its head,
As I skip through dreams, completely misled.

A parrot squawks out, "What's the plan?"
I wink and say, "I'm just a fan!"
While logic stews in a mental pot,
I find my rhythm in what's forgot.

So join the dance, let worries fade,
In laughter's arms, we're all remade.
Let's jive on doubts and waltz through fears,
For life's a show, with laughs and cheers.

Heartbeats of the Unsought

In flames of chance, I dance with fate,
Each stumble's cherished, never too late.
A clown with dreams beyond attach,
In joy's disguise, life's a patchwork match.

Invisible strings pull at my heart,
Yet laughter bubbles—a crucial part.
In every twist, a chuckle's made,
For why know why? Just dive in and wade.

The doorbell rings—who could it be?
A pizza man with jokes for me!
We feast on smiles and share a laugh,
In this absurd, rather odd craft.

So when the questions loom and pry,
Take a leap, let your spirit fly.
In silliness found, the answers glow,
So dance a jig, and let love flow.

The Stillness of Uncertainty

In a world that spins with glee,
I sip my tea, what will be will be.
Flip a coin, heads or tails,
Confidence comes on tiny sails.

Walking blind on winding roads,
With mismatched socks, I bear my loads.
Dance with doubt, let laughter reign,
Jump in puddles, embrace the rain.

Painting in Hues of Doubt

Brush in hand, I smear the sky,
With colors bright and questions nigh.
A canvas filled with swirling lies,
Yet I laugh with joyful sighs.

Throw in some polka dots of dread,
Mixing all shades of green and red.
Art may not reveal a clue,
But it's fun to make a mess, it's true!

Starlight in the Dark

Stars waltz in the velvet night,
While I chase fireflies in flight.
Questions twinkle, dance and tease,
I trip on laughter, oh what a breeze!

Mismatched shoes on my happy feet,
Life's a riddle, oh so sweet.
If I can't see the end's bright glow,
I'll twirl with shadows, and steal the show.

Serene Acceptance of the Unfamiliar

In a room with chairs askew,
I sit and ponder the odd view.
Laughing with ghosts of yesterday,
They tell me silly games to play.

Embrace the chaos, wiggle and sway,
Who cares what others say today?
Life's a jigsaw, missing parts,
Yet, it's stitched together with open hearts.

Accepting the Great Unknown

In a world where answers flee,
We juggle life like clowns, you see.
Questions dance, while wisdom hides,
We ride the waves, on silly tides.

With socks that clash and hair askew,
We plan our meals, but call them stew.
Maps that lead us straight to bliss,
What's funnier, a yes or this?

The stars above play peek-a-boo,
We toast to dreams that might come true.
In confusing fogs, we skip and trip,
Life's a laugh, a nonsensical script.

So let's embrace the mystery,
With every giggle a victory.
To stumble through without a clue,
Is the best kind of to-do for you!

Whispers of the Unknowable

The clock ticks loud, but time's a trick,
With every tick, we play a pick.
Whispers float on winds of fate,
Why's the answer to be late?

Like socks that vanish in the wash,
We ponder big, yet dance with posh.
What is truth? A question's song,
In this odd world, we all belong.

A mystery wrapped in riddle's guise,
We eat our cake, and wear our ties.
With plans that fizzle, jokes that soar,
Life's humor knocks on every door.

So whisper low to silence bold,
Sing with giggles, let hearts unfold.
In the unknowable, joy does thrive,
We laugh and leap, all the way alive!

Revelations in Silence

Amidst the noise, there's quiet cheer,
A sneaky smile, the truth appears.
In moments still, we find our pace,
Life's a puzzle, we misplace.

Why did the chicken cross the road?
The answer's lost, a funny ode.
Like cats that plot and dogs that scheme,
We chase our tales, a silly dream.

In empty rooms, we hear the laughs,
With echoes of our goofy gaffs.
So let's embrace the jokes we've spun,
In a laughing life, we've already won!

Through revelations in silent grace,
We dance unknowing, with a winking face.
Each giggle shared makes doubts rewind,
In this riotous world, we're perfectly aligned!

Trusting the Unwritten Script

The stage is set, yet lines unclear,
In this comedy, there's nothing to fear.
With quirky hats and shoes from two,
We strut through scenes, a grand debut.

Our scripts are scribbles, jokes up high,
We play our parts as life draws nigh.
Trust the chaos, it's part of the game,
What's funny is, we're all the same.

The plot twists wildly, laughs compete,
With banana peels beneath our feet.
So shrug your shoulders, take a chance,
In this unwritten life, let's dance!

To trust the script that's yet unsaid,
Is to weave joy from fears we've bred.
In every laugh, the truth ignites,
Living funny in unwritten nights!

The Unknown Blooms in Quiet Moments

In a world where questions dance,
We step with every glance.
We chuckle at the silly sights,
While sipping tea on starry nights.

With every turn, a puzzle's born,
Like socks that vanish, freshly worn.
We laugh at life's absurd parade,
As cats defy the laws we've made.

The clock ticks on in playful jest,
While pondering a nap is best.
We wander through the foggy haze,
And giggle at our crazy ways.

In silent moments, doubts emit,
Yet somehow, we're okay with it.
For who needs answers, clear and neat,
When life's surprise is oh-so sweet?

A Song for the Unknowing

Oh dear, what's this? A brand new game,
With nary a clue, but it's all the same.
We dance with riddles, oh what a show,
As umbrellas bloom in the winter snow.

We sing our tunes in offbeat time,
Like squirrels attempting to mimic a rhyme.
Each note a guess, a cheerful cheer,
As wisdom giggles, just out of ear.

The weather changes, who is to say?
A sunburn in winter, come what may.
With every step, the jokes we weave,
In moments we typically wouldn't believe.

So lift your glass to the great unknown,
With clinks and laughs, you're not alone.
In this melody of goofy bliss,
Embrace the fumbles, and all will be missed!

Portraits of Uncertainty

There's a painting hanging, brushstrokes wide,
With colors splattered that something tried.
Each stroke's a question, bold and bright,
Like squirrels on bicycles, what a sight!

Uncertain faces peer from the frame,
All wearing hats, yet none the same.
With winks and grins, they play pretend,
While mysteries twist and never end.

They juggle pickles, they twirl around,
While laughter echoes, a whimsical sound.
For every guess, a riddle spins,
As life's merry chase in chaos begins.

So here's to the odd, the quirky and brave,
The portraits of life wherein we misbehave.
With every chuckle, a truth unfolds,
In the art of not knowing, a story is told.

Reaching for Horizons Beyond

In a rocket made of cardboard dreams,
We soar through realms and popping seams.
With marshmallow clouds as our steering aids,
We giggle at the strange charades.

With eyes wide open to nothing clear,
We toast to the future, with cups of cheer.
For who can tell what lies ahead,
When jellybeans float over our heads?

We fish for stars in a lemonade sea,
While mapping paths for you and me.
Each leap feels sure, though slightly bent,
In the quest for answers, we're happily spent.

So wave your flag at the silly fate,
For every misstep, we'll celebrate.
In the realms of whimsy, we'll find a way,
Embracing the unknown, come what may!

Embracing the Blank Canvas

I painted my dreams with colors bright,
But forgot what color is the sky at night.
I splash and I dash with a brush in hand,
Yet every stroke leads to a house of sand.

When life gives you lemons, just dance away,
Who needs a recipe for the perfect day?
With paint on my face and a grin so wide,
I laugh at the blankness, my canvas, my guide.

I sometimes forget why I'm here at all,
But jokes fill the gaps like a fun-loving wall.
If questions arise, I just shrug my shoulders,
Life's better with giggles as my biggest boulders.

So here's to the chaos, the mess, and the cheer,
Life's an adventure—let's make it unclear!
We'll paint it together, no reason required,
In the humor of wondering, we'll never get tired.

Laughter Among the Shadows

In the corners of night where the shadows might creep,
I chuckle and whisper, and giggle in sleep.
With a tickle from dreams that flutter and play,
I waltz through the darkness, not fearing the sway.

The moon gives a wink as it chases my fright,
"I'm just here for comedy," it calls out tonight.
In the shadows, I find all my unexpected joys,
By laughing at ghosts, like mischievous boys.

If answers are hiding in towers of doubt,
I'll juggle my worries and dance all about.
"Who needs the answers?" I'll shout to the sky,
When laughter's the compass, I'm free to glide by.

So let the shadows play tag with the light,
They spark all my jokes, and they're always polite.
With chuckles and giggles, my life's a delight,
Among laughter and shadows, I'm never out of sight.

The Path Less Understood

There's a path in the woods where I wander each day,
It twists and it tangles, it leads me astray.
With a sign that says "detour" all covered in moss,
I chuckle and think of the paths that I toss.

I trip on my thoughts like a cat on a kite,
And the squirrels laugh out loud—oh, what a sight!
"Why not follow the chaos? It's full of delight!"
Says a rabbit with glasses, munching on light.

In the fog of confusion, I wear my best grin,
While pondering how such nonsense can win.
Each twist is a tickle, each stumble a cheer,
I dance through the questions while drinking my beer.

So raise up your glass to the unknown ahead,
To laughter and wonder and all that's unsaid.
For the path less understood is a journey, you see,
Filled with fun, frolic, and no sense of plea.

Mindfulness in the Abyss

In the deep of the void where the mind likes to drift,
I meditate wildly, a comical gift.
With thoughts floating by like balloons in the breeze,
I smile at the nonsense that's sure to appease.

"Why ponder the reason?" the echoes will say,
As I skip down this path in a whimsical way.
With feet made of giggles and eyes full of cheer,
I invite in the chaos, it's just good to be here.

I juggle my worries like cats in a hat,
While the universe chuckles and flicks at my spat.
"Existence is funny!" I'll gladly proclaim,
As I dance on the edge of my own silly game.

So here's to the abyss, so grand and profound,
With laughter and tickles forever abound.
For in this sweet madness, my spirit takes flight,
Mindfulness sparkles, my heart feels just right.

Through Fog and Ambiguity

In the morning mist, we stride,
Chasing shadows that hide inside.
With coffee dreams and socks that clash,
We stumble forward, making a splash.

The compass spins, the map's a joke,
A rubber chicken's our only hope.
We laugh at clouds that block the sun,
And dance like fools, 'cause it's more fun.

Light in the Absence of Reasons

With a flashlight that flickers, we find our way,
Through wild antics and a cat's ballet.
For every question, we shout 'Why not?'
Bumper stickers say, 'Who cares? Just trot!'

Our reason's lost, but we sing aloud,
With pop songs that make us feel quite proud.
We juggle lemons and forget the rest,
In the circus of life, we're truly blessed.

When Secrets Stay Silent

The whispers hide in corners tight,
Where socks go missing in the night.
We wear our hats on backwards, see,
Embracing chaos, wild and free.

Our secrets dance like a chicken's waddle,
In a world of mystery, we all just twaddle.
So raise a glass to the things unsaid,
And toss confetti in our heads!

The Beauty of Unanswered Dreams

A kite without string floats high and wide,
In a game where the rules we all deride.
We paint rainbows with invisible ink,
And laugh at the logic we didn't think.

Chasing stars with glittery shoes,
We embrace the silly and refuse to lose.
In every question, there's joy to find,
In the beautifully vague, we're all aligned.